Fairy Tale Science

Making a Pulley System for Rapunzel

by Nikole Brooks Bethea

FOCUS
READERS®

BEACON

www.focusreaders.com

Focus Readers is distributed by North Star Editions:
sales@northstareditions.com | 888-417-0195

Produced for Focus Readers by Red Line Editorial.

Photographs ©: Niday Picture Library/Alamy, cover (left), 1 (left); Red Line Editorial, cover (right), 1 (right), 11, 13, 15, 17, 25; firina/iStockphoto, 4; Vladimir Vinogradov/iStockphoto, 7; kjschraa/iStockphoto, 8, 29; M88/Shutterstock Images, 18; WitR/Shutterstock Images, 21; Zerbor/Shutterstock Images, 22; VanDenEsker/iStockphoto, 27

Library of Congress Cataloging-in-Publication Data
Names: Bethea, Nikole Brooks, author.
Title: Making a pulley system for Rapunzel / by Nikole Brooks Bethea.
Description: Lake Elmo, MN : Focus Readers, 2020. | Series: Fairy tale science | Includes index. | Audience: Grades 4–6.
Identifiers: LCCN 2019032152 (print) | LCCN 2019032153 (ebook) | ISBN 9781644930298 (hardcover) | ISBN 9781644931080 (paperback) | ISBN 9781644932667 (pdf) | ISBN 9781644931875 (ebook)
Subjects: LCSH: Pulleys--Juvenile literature. | Rapunzel (Tale)--Juvenile literature.
Classification: LCC TJ1103 .B49 2020 (print) | LCC TJ1103 (ebook) | DDC 621.8--dc23
LC record available at https://lccn.loc.gov/2019032152
LC ebook record available at https://lccn.loc.gov/2019032153

Printed in the United States of America
Mankato, MN
012020

About the Author

Nikole Brooks Bethea is a licensed professional engineer. She earned bachelor's and master's degrees in environmental engineering from the University of Florida, and she worked as a professional engineer for 15 years. Bethea has written more than 35 science and engineering books for children.

Table of Contents

Chapter 1

The Story of Rapunzel

A couple wanted food from a witch's garden. So, the husband took some food. But the witch caught him. She punished them by taking their new baby. The witch named the child Rapunzel.

 The husband stole food from the witch's garden.

She locked Rapunzel inside a
tall tower.

Years later, a prince heard music
coming from the tower. He looked
for a door. But there was none.
So, he hid and waited. The witch
came. She called for Rapunzel to let
down her hair. Rapunzel's long hair
draped from the tower window. The
witch climbed up her hair.

Later, the prince called to
Rapunzel. He climbed up her hair.
But the witch found out. She cut

 Rapunzel's tower could not be entered except through a high window.

Rapunzel's hair. Then she sent the girl away.

The prince returned to the tower. He called to Rapunzel. He climbed up the hair. But it was the witch in the tower instead. The prince leaped from the tower to escape.

Chapter 2

Make a Pulley

To enter the tower, the prince had to climb Rapunzel's hair. But he could have used a **pulley** instead. This simple machine makes it easier to lift things.

 A pulley would have helped the prince enter the tower.

You will build a simple pulley for the prince. The **design** uses household items. An adult should supervise the use of the sharpened pencil.

Materials

- 1 tall, cylindrical can (such as that used for potato chips or tennis balls)
- Rocks or other small, heavy objects to weigh down the can
- 1 sharpened pencil
- 2 clothespins

- 24 inches (61 cm) of yarn or string

- 1 small paper cup

- 1 pipe cleaner

- Several coins

Instructions

1. Pick up the pencil. Gently poke two small holes near the top of the paper cup. The holes should be on opposite sides of the cup.

2. Thread the pipe cleaner through both holes. Curve both ends of the pipe cleaner upward. Twist

Many old water wells used pulleys. People could lower a bucket into the well. They could raise the bucket filled with water.

the two ends together. The cup

will be your bucket.

3. Tie one end of the yarn to the

pipe cleaner.

4. Place the rocks into the tall can.

The weight will keep the can

from tipping over.

5. Clip the two clothespins to the top of the can. They should be about 1 inch (2.5 cm) apart.

6. Place the pencil across the clothespins.

7. Loop the loose end of the yarn over the pencil. It should rest between the two clothespins. Gently pull down on the yarn. The bucket will lift.

8. Add a coin to the bucket to make it heavier. Test the pulley. Pull down on the yarn.

9. Keep adding coins until the design fails. For example, the can may tip over. The clothespins may snap off. The pencil may fall. Count the number of coins this design can lift without failing.

Elevators

Elevators are examples of pulleys in action. The elevator car connects to strong, metal **cables**. The cables wrap around wheels. The wheels are far above the car. An electric **motor** pulls the cables. This movement pulls the car up.

Normally, the motor would need to lift the car's full weight. But elevators use a **counterweight**. This weight balances the car's weight. When the elevator goes up, the counterweight goes down. When the elevator lowers, the counterweight rises. The counterweight makes it easier for the motor to lift the car's weight. The motor only needs to lift the difference between the two weights.

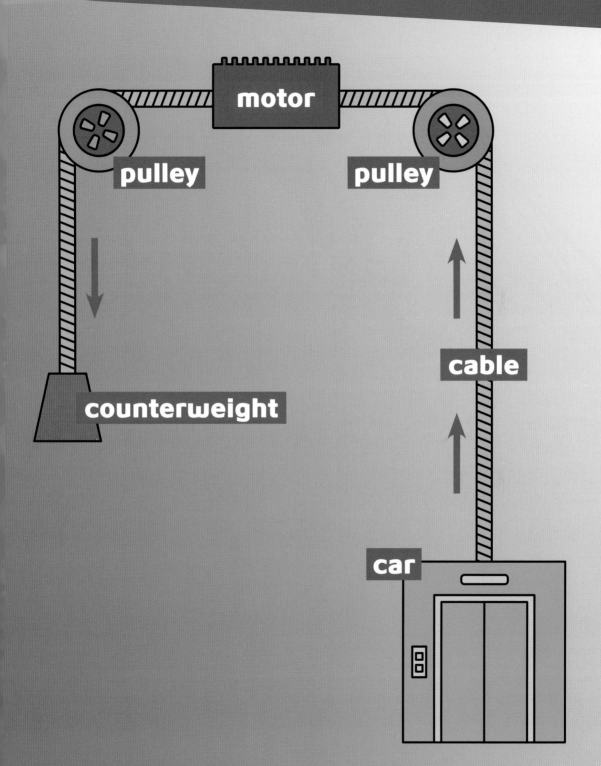

motor

pulley

pulley

counterweight

cable

car

Chapter 3

Results

Pulleys help people lift heavy **loads**. In this activity, the load was the bucket. You pulled down on one end of the yarn. This motion lifted the other end of the yarn. It also lifted the attached bucket.

Cranes use pulley systems to lift heavy loads.

The pulley changed a downward **force** into an upward one.

Adjust your design to improve the pulley. Try some of these ideas:

- Add more rocks to the can to better hold it in place.
- Use tape or paper clips to hold the clothespins in place.

Fun Fact

Some scientists think the ancient Egyptians used pulleys. Pulleys could explain how they lifted large stones to build the pyramids.

 Simple machines such as pulleys may have helped ancient Egyptians build the pyramids.

- Replace the pencil with a different cylindrical object. You might use an empty thread spool or a wooden chopstick.

- Try making a pulley with different materials. Create a new design. Record the number of coins each design lifts.

Chapter 4

How Pulleys Work

Pulleys are simple machines. They are made of a wheel and a rope. The wheel has a **groove** in it. The rope loops around the wheel. It lies in the groove.

 The wheel spins when the rope is pulled.

Simple machines change the size or direction of a force. Forces are pushes or pulls. They can change the motion of an object. They can also change its direction. For example, the wind pushing a sailboat is a force. Gravity is another force. It pulls objects down to the ground.

Fun Fact

Theaters use pulley systems. The pulleys raise and lower the stage curtains.

Types of Pulleys

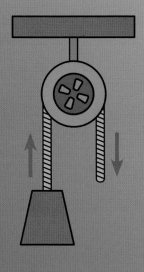

Fixed pulleys remain in one place.

Movable pulleys move. Pulling the rope lifts the wheel along with the load.

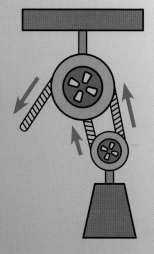

Compound pulleys combine pulleys. Pulling the rope around one pulley lifts the second pulley.

People lift objects by using force. A pulley can make lifting a heavy object easier. It does this by changing the direction of the force.

One example is a flagpole. A pulley sits at the top of the flagpole. People pull the rope down on one side of the pole. The pulley's wheel spins. The flag lifts on the other side of the pole. People use a downward force. But the force lifting the flag is an upward one.

Fun Fact

Several pulleys can be combined. The pulleys work together. They make loads even easier to lift.

 People can raise and lower flags using pulleys.

Pulleys can be found all around. A pull cord wraps around pulleys to raise and lower blinds. Some clotheslines use pulleys. Cranes at construction sites also use pulleys.

FOCUS ON
Making a Pulley System

Write your answers on a separate piece of paper.

1. Write a paragraph describing how a pulley works.

2. Where else might pulleys be useful in the real world?

3. Why does pulling a cord raise a flag up a pole?
   - **A.** The pulley changes the size of the force.
   - **B.** The pulley changes the direction of the force.
   - **C.** The pulley lessens the pull of gravity on the flag.

4. What would have to be changed in an elevator's design if there was no counterweight?
   - **A.** The motor would need to be more powerful.
   - **B.** The pulleys would no longer be needed.
   - **C.** Less force would be needed to lift the elevator.

5. What does **draped** mean in this book?

*She called for Rapunzel to let down her hair. Rapunzel's long hair **draped** from the tower window. The witch climbed up her hair.*

    A. covered

    B. lifted up

    C. fell loosely

6. What does **balances** mean in this book?

*This weight **balances** the car's weight. When the elevator goes up, the counterweight goes down. When the elevator lowers, the counterweight rises.*

    A. adds onto the weight of

    B. opposes with an equal force

    C. reduces the weight of

Answer key on page 32.

Glossary

cables
Thick, strong wire ropes.

counterweight
A weight or force used to balance another weight or force.

design
A drawing or plan for a project.

force
A push or pull that one object has on another.

groove
A long, narrow cut or channel.

loads
Masses or weights supported by something.

motor
A machine that changes electricity into mechanical energy, or motion.

pulley
A wheel with a groove that a rope or chain runs through.

To Learn More

BOOKS

Alkire, Jessie. *Construct It! Architecture You Can Build, Break, and Build Again*. Minneapolis: Abdo Publishing, 2018.

Felix, Rebecca. *Cool Engineering Projects: Fun & Creative Workshop Activities*. Minneapolis: Abdo Publishing, 2017.

Swanson, Jennifer. *Explore Forces and Motion!* White River Junction, VT: Nomad Press, 2016.

NOTE TO EDUCATORS

Visit **www.focusreaders.com** to find lesson plans, activities, links, and other resources related to this title.

Index

C
counterweight, 16–17

E
elevators, 16

F
flagpole, 26
forces, 20, 24–26

L
loads, 19, 25, 26

R
Rapunzel, 5–7, 9
rope, 23, 25, 26

S
simple machines, 9, 23–24

W
water wells, 12
wheels, 16, 23, 25, 26